What is ORGANIC Chemistry?

Chemistry Book 4th Grade

Children's Chemistry Books

Speedy Publishing LLC
40 E. Main St. #1156
Newark, DE 19711
www.speedypublishing.com

All living creatures on our Earth are organisms. When we study them, we study how they live and act, but we can also study how their bodies work. That second part is what organic chemistry is all about. Let's find out what we can learn!

WHAT'S ORGANIC CHEMISTRY?

Living creatures live because their bodies carry out processes. They take in nutrients and other things the animal, insect, or plant needs to survive. They process those resources so the body can use them. They keep themselves healthy. They have children so the species can continue. And they get rid of what the body can't use.

water drop from leaf and laboratory
for natural chemistry concept

Green housefly on leaf

The study of how plants, animals, and insects manage these process- es is called organic chemistry. Organic chemistry is what lets living things on the Earth function.

CARBON IS THE KEY

The focus of organic chemistry is on carbon molecules. Carbon atoms are essential to life as we know it, and also to many other substances.

Carbon is different from most other elements. Its atoms can combine into very complex molecules that might involve hundreds or even thousands of individual carbon atoms. This means there are many, many carbon compounds, based on those molecules. In fact, there are more carbon compounds than there are compounds of all the other elements put together.

Diamond nestled in bedrock

Carbon atoms have four electrons in their outer shell. This means each atom can bond (share an electron) with four other atoms.

The other important thing about carbon atoms is that they pack together tightly. Diamonds, a highly-compressed form of carbon, are so strong because their atoms are so tightly packed together and linked to each other.

CARBON COMPOUNDS

Carbon, combined with just a few other elements, can make many different compounds depending on how many atoms of each element there are and how they are arranged. The most useful elements that combine with carbon are nitrogen, oxygen, and hydrogen.

SET OF CHEMICAL AND PHYSICAL ATOMS/MOLECULES MODELS OF OXYGEN, HYDROGEN AND CARBON AND THEIR JOININGS. DIOXIDE GAS. METHANE. ETHANE.

Oxygen

Hydrogen

Carbon

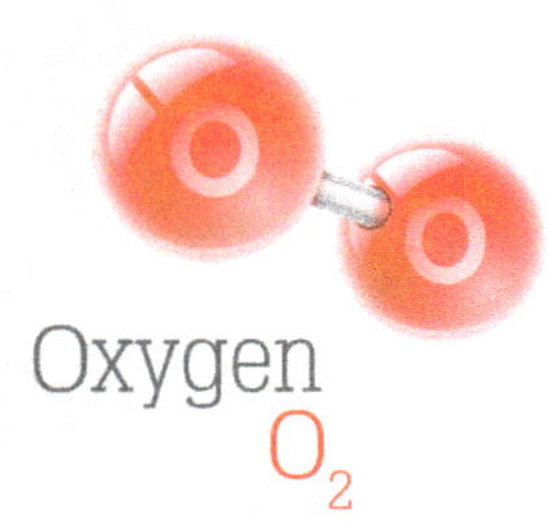

Oxygen
O_2

Hydrogen
H_2

Water
H_2O

Carbon
dioxide
CO_2

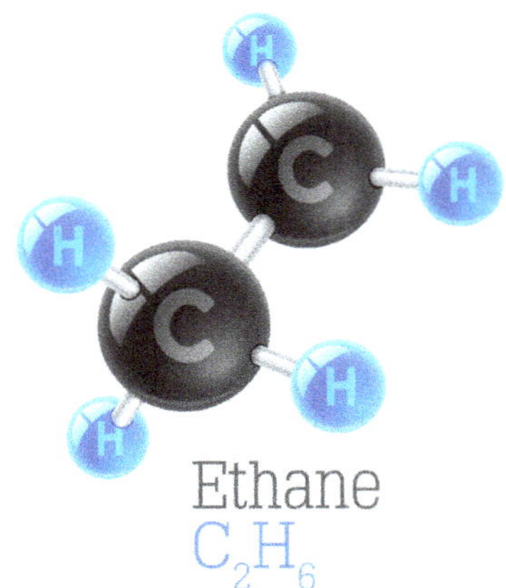

Ethane
C_2H_6

Methane
CH_4

HYDROCARBONS IN AN OIL DROP

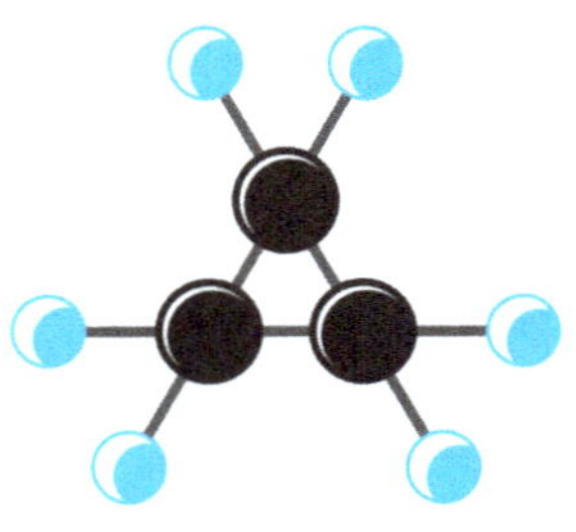

cyclopropane

C3H6

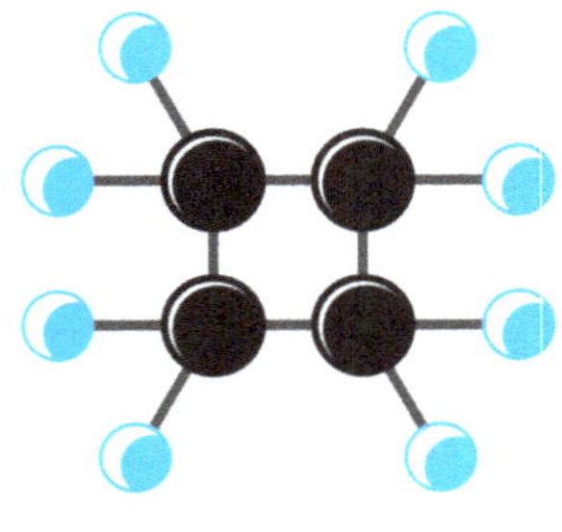

cyclobutane

C4H8

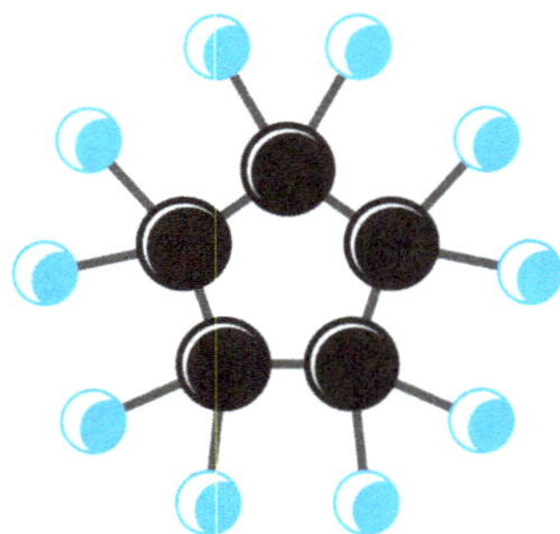

cyclopentane

C5H10

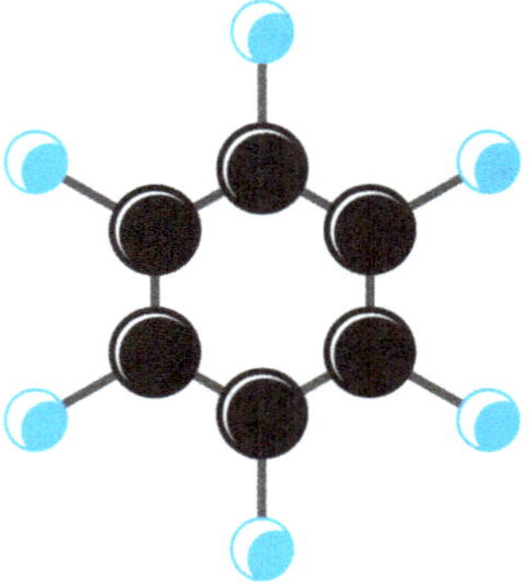

cyclohexane

C6H12

benzene

C6H6

Carbon atoms can join with hydrogen atoms in chains (long sets of connections) called hydrocarbons. These are the basis of the oil, gas, and other fossil fuels we burn.

CARBON REACTIVITY

Reactivity, simply, is how quickly a carbon compound reacts to its environment: to how hot it is, to whatever other chemicals are around it, to the pressure being applied to it, and so on. In general, a longer carbon chain makes a less chemically reactive compound than a shorter chain does.

serotonin formule
$C_{10}H_{12}N_2O$

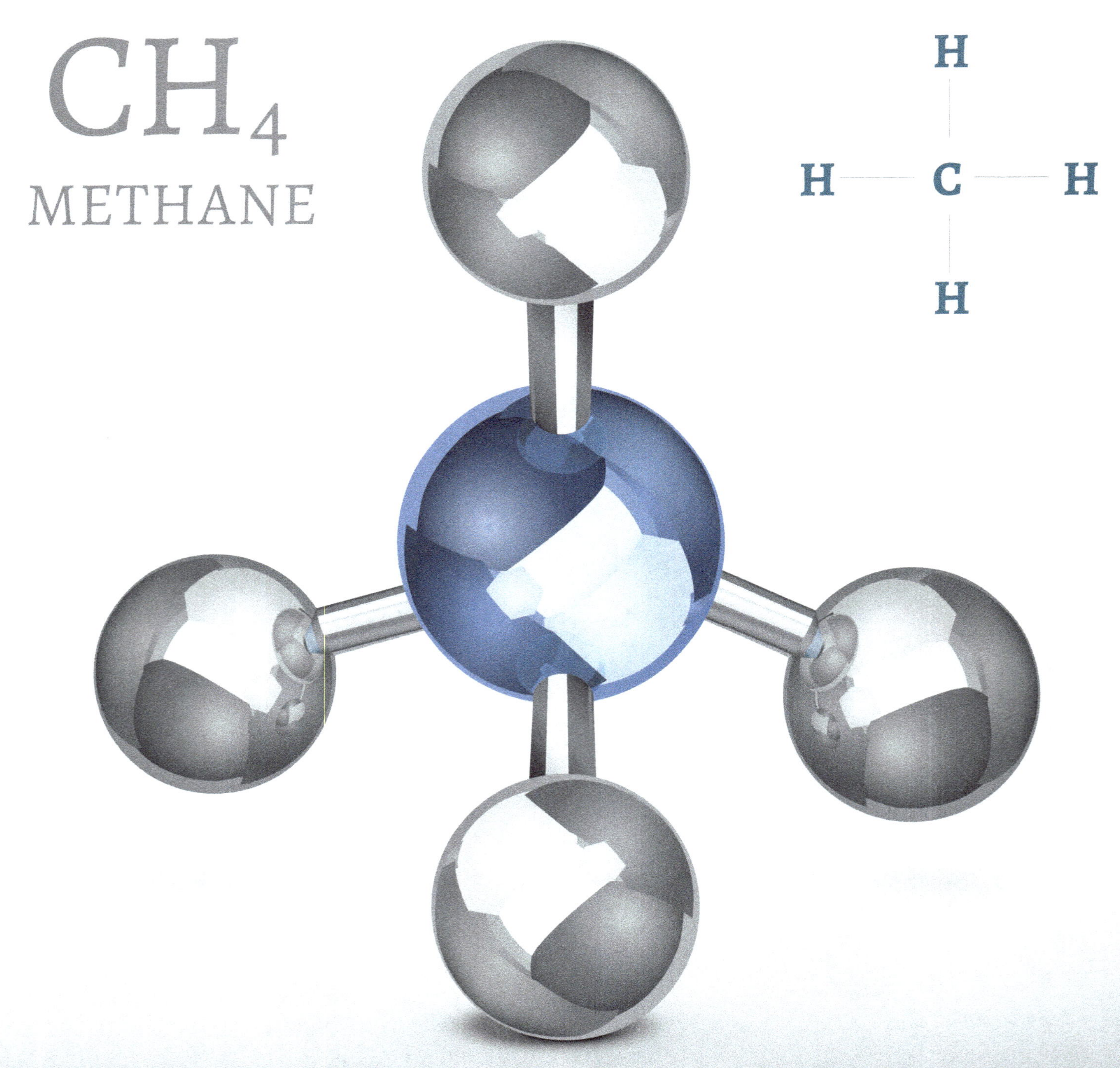

CH4
METHANE
H
H C H
H

MELTING AND BOILING

If the melting and boiling points of a compound are high, then it is less reactive. If the melting and boiling points are lower, the compound is more reactive.

For example, methane is a hydrocarbon and the main element in natural gas. It has just one carbon and four hydrogen atoms in each of its molecules, which is the shortest of the carbon compounds. The boiling point of methane is very low, -162 degrees Celsius, so it is highly reactive and is a gas at room temperature.

A compound that has a very long carbon chain might have a very high boiling point, well above the 100 degrees Celsius at which water boils. Such a compound would not be a gas at room temperature, and we would say it is less reactive.

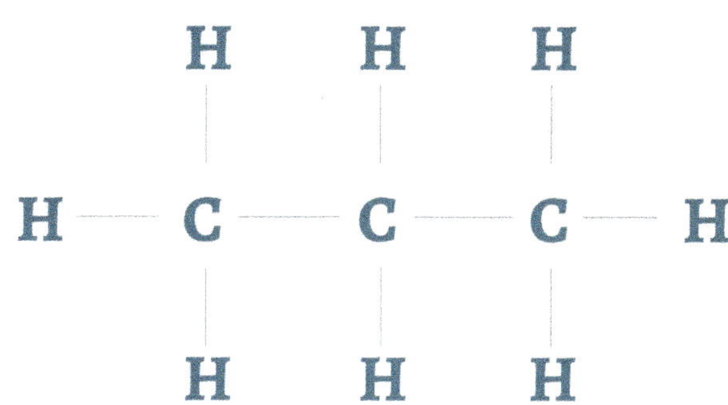

C₃H₈
PROPANE
H H H
H-C-C-C-H
H H H

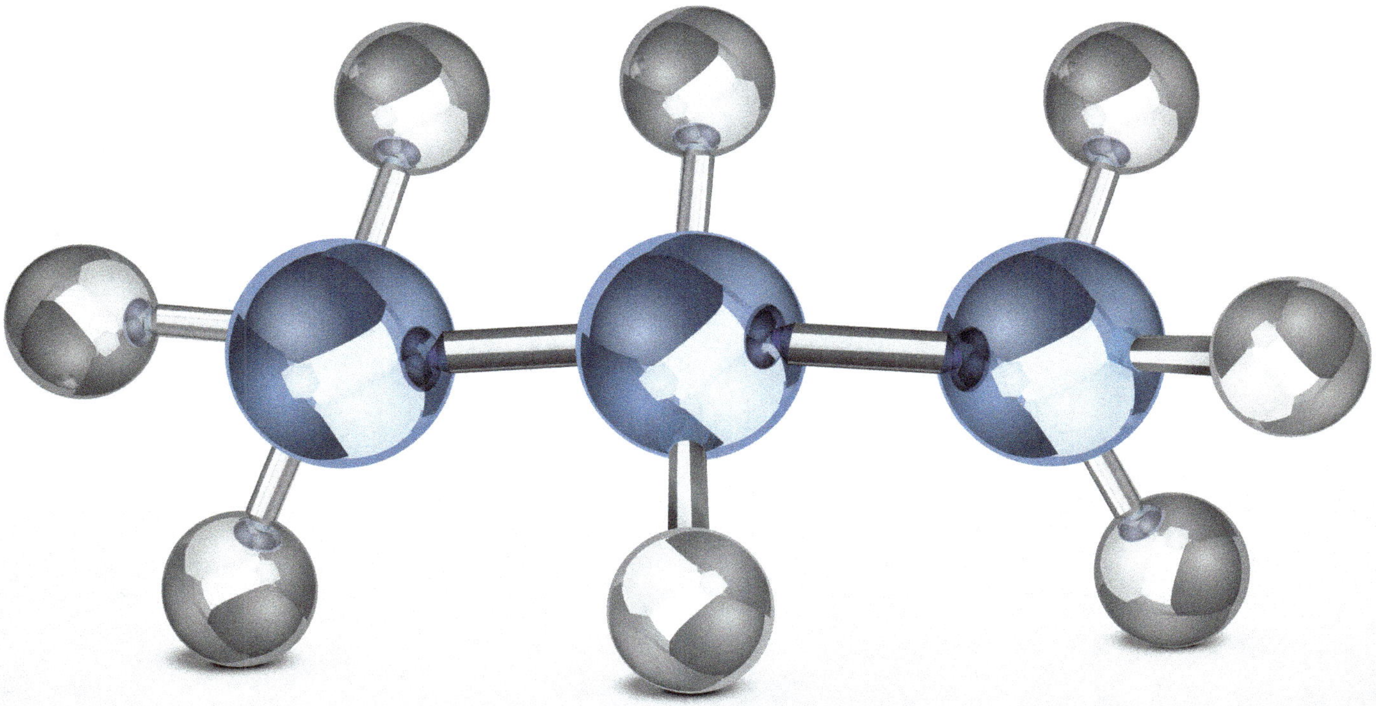

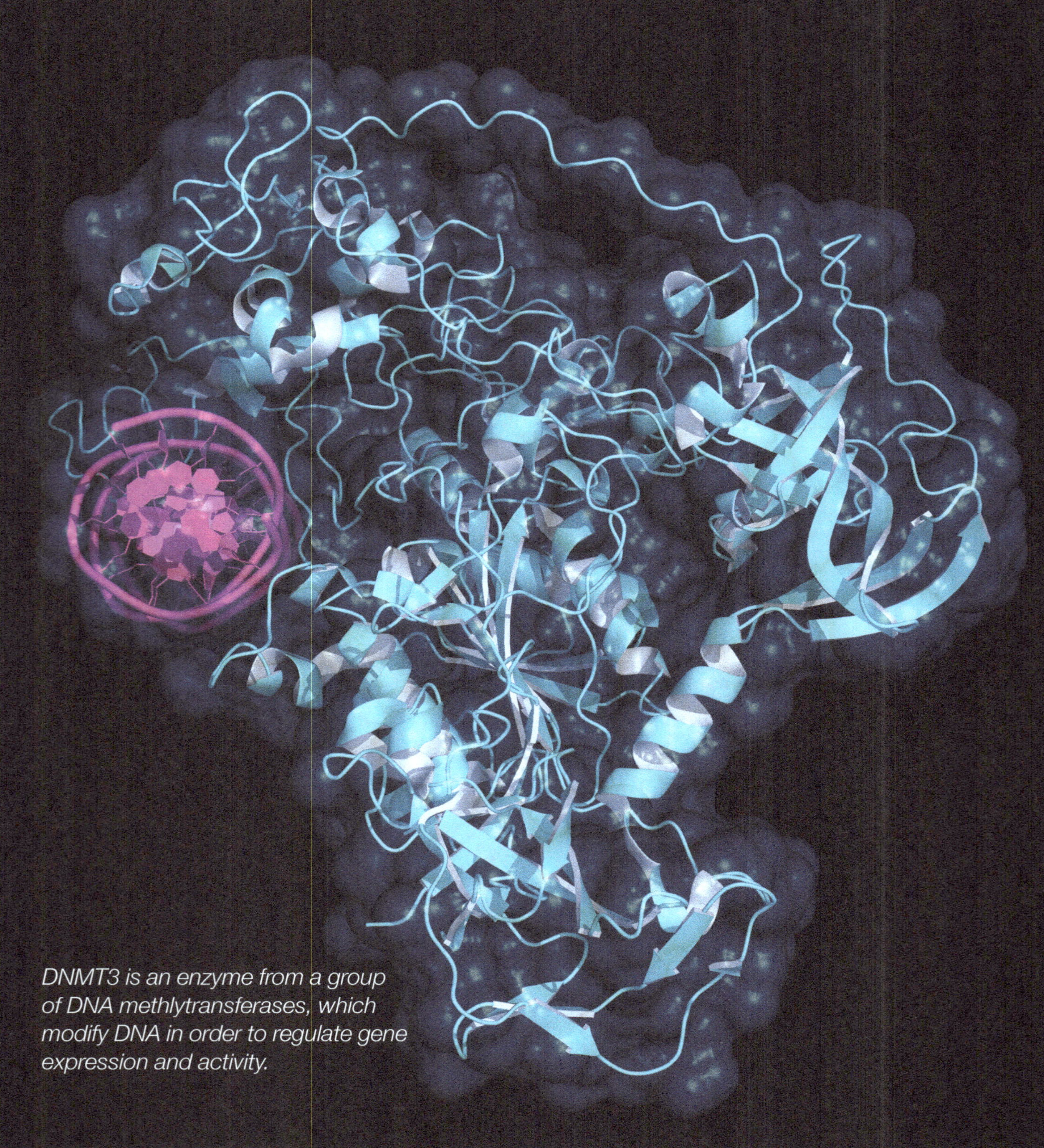

DNMT3 is an enzyme from a group
of DNA methlytransferases, which
modify DNA in order to regulate gene
expression and activity.

IT ISN'T JUST THE HEAT

However, in carbon-based molecules in living creatures, other things than just chemical action are at work. For instance, enzymes may be working on the compound to break it down into smaller bits that the cells can use.

FUNCTIONAL GROUPS

Scientists group molecules together if their physical or chemical properties are similar. This makes it easier to understand what is the same and what is different among the members of a functional group.

Molecular Model

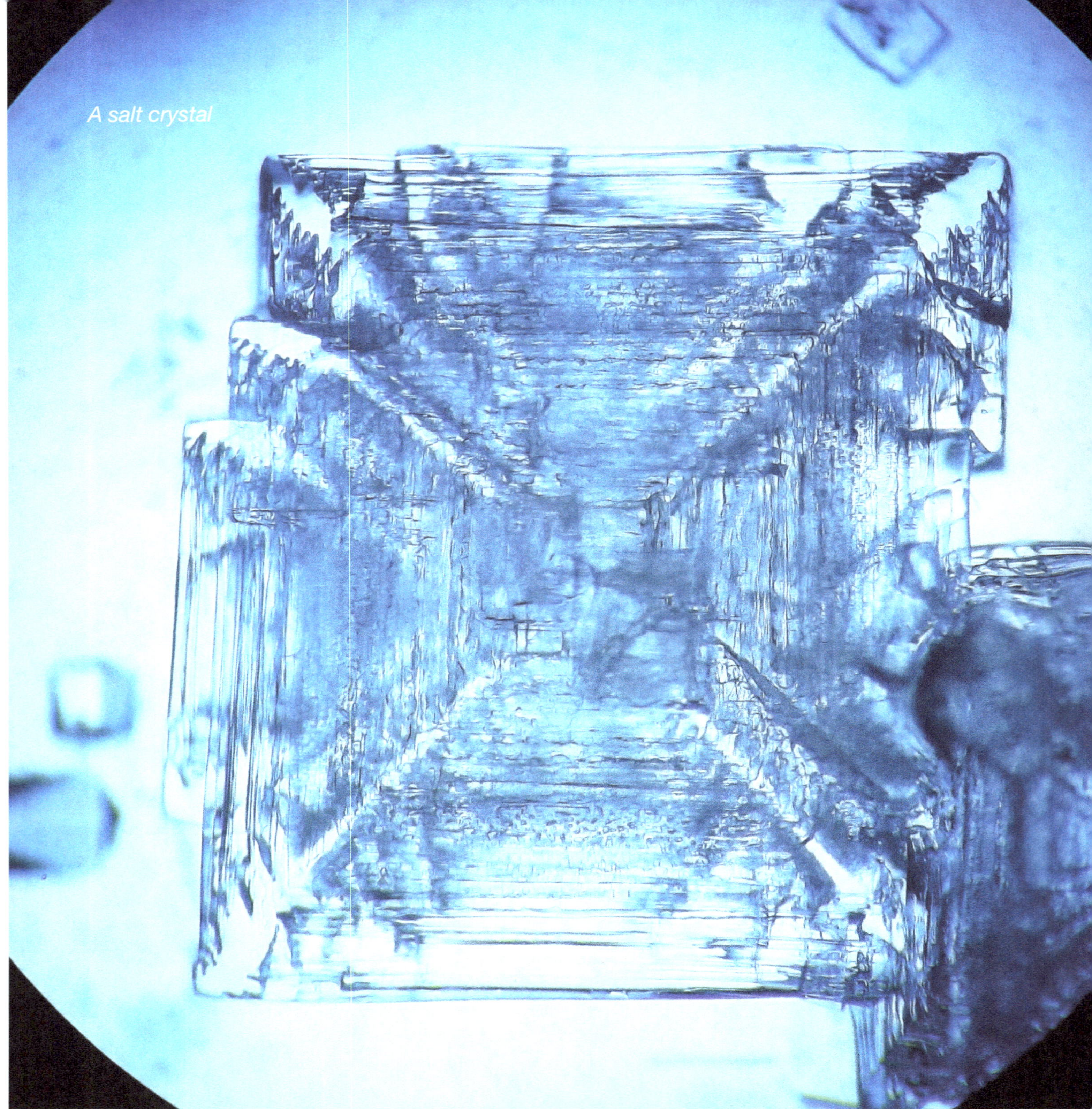
A salt crystal

Function groups can have different grouping methods:

CHEMICAL PROPERTIES

A group of molecules that react to a chemical by changing to another substance have a similar chemical property. When you mix sodium with chlorine gas, the result is a new substance, sodium chloride. We also call this "table salt", and you probably eat some of it every day!

PHYSICAL PROPERTIES

You might group substances by how they react to physical events, like pressure. They may break into smaller parts of the same substance, but they don't change chemically.

Salt crystal

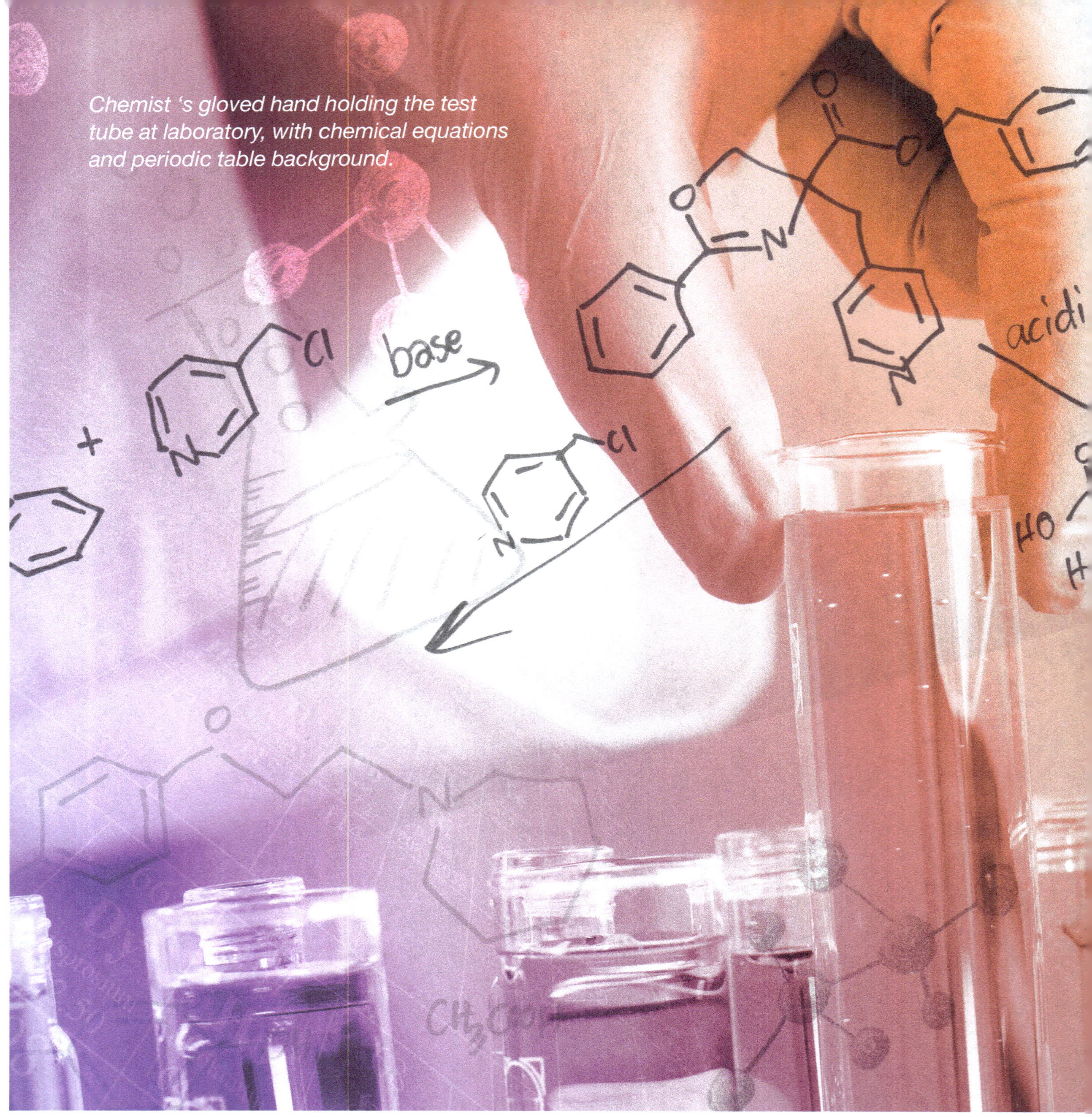

Chemist 's gloved hand holding the test tube at laboratory, with chemical equations and periodic table background.
base
acidi
Cl
Cl
HO
H
CH₃COOH

POLARITY AND ACIDITY

Some functional groups are based on whether its members are acidic, neutral, or basic. Some molecules have a magnetic charge at one end (the polar end) and no charge at the other end.

CARBON IN LIVING THINGS

A single carbon atom can combine with up to four other atoms. When carbon forms organic compounds, they can be quite complex and involve many molecules, which themselves are made up of many atoms.

Large, complex compounds are what carry the nutrients, cell information, and other resources that living cells need to understand what they are to do, and to do it.

Cell structure of a leaf

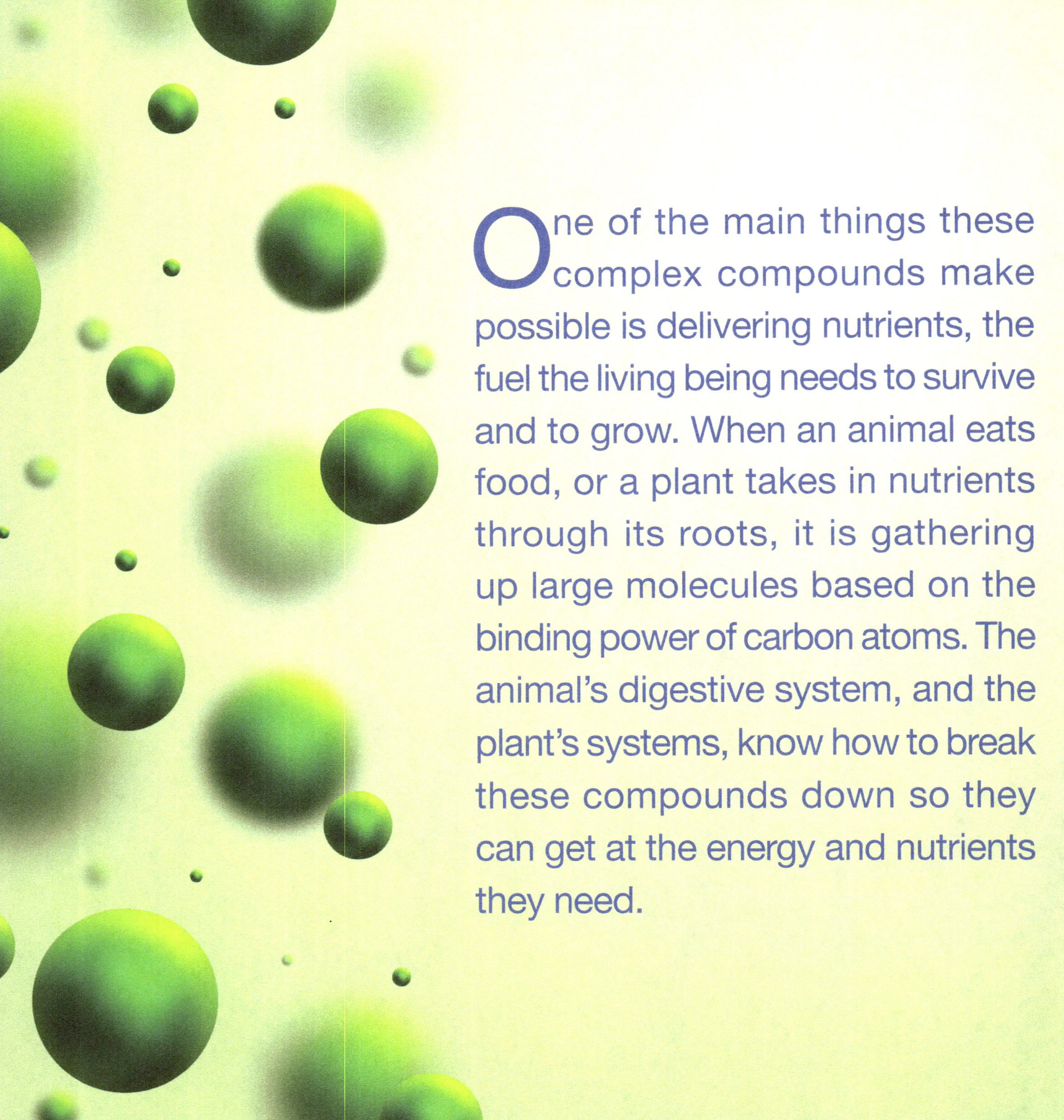

One of the main things these complex compounds make possible is delivering nutrients, the fuel the living being needs to survive and to grow. When an animal eats food, or a plant takes in nutrients through its roots, it is gathering up large molecules based on the binding power of carbon atoms. The animal's digestive system, and the plant's systems, know how to break these compounds down so they can get at the energy and nutrients they need.

The energy and nutrients enter the cells of the plant or animal, and within each cell there are other large molecules that know what to do with them.

WHY AN APPLE SMELLS LIKE AN APPLE

When we sniff an apple, it smells sweet and tasty. Why is that? Apples have a carbon compound called an ester, and when bits of that compound reach your nose, they give you that pleasant smell.

When acid and alcohol work on each other, they can make an ester. An ester molecule is made up of carbon, oxygen, and hydrogen atoms.

Ripe apples

CARBON IN NON-LIVING THINGS

Carbon is the key in the makeup of these non-living substances in our world:

METHANE

Methane is a natural gas, and we use it a lot for heating and for the fuel for big machines. Methane has one carbon atom connected, or bonded, to four hydrogen atoms.

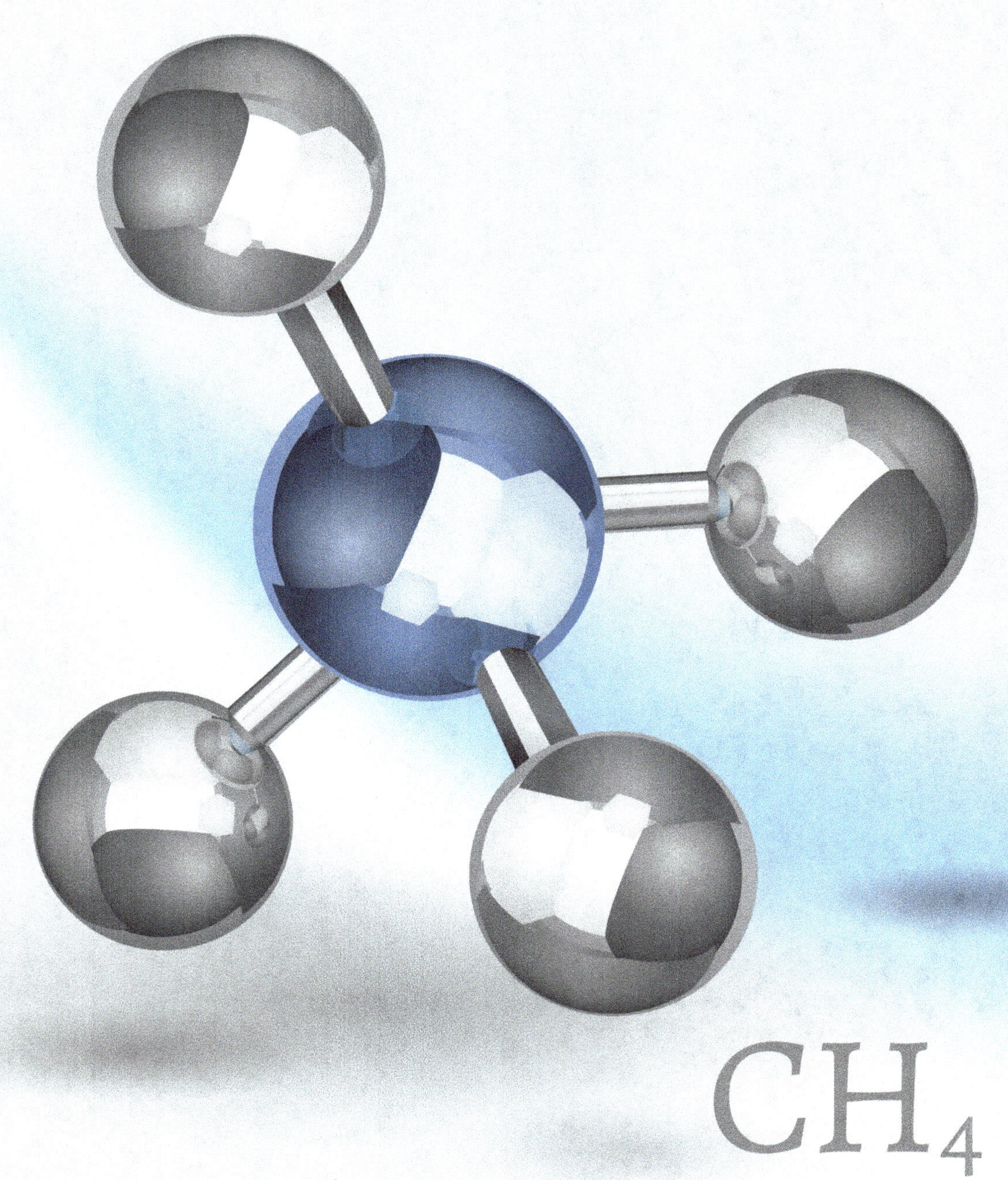
METHANE MOLECULES
CH$_4$

BUTANE MOLECULE

C_4H_{10}

BUTANE

Butane is another burnable substance. A butane molecule has four carbon atoms bonded to ten hydrogen atoms in a chain.

BENZENE

A ring of six carbon atoms, each bonded to a hydrogen atom, makes benzene. We use it as a gas when we make colorful dyes and pigments.

Compounds where the carbon atoms form a ring are called aromatics. Scientists call them that because of their noticeable smell. When we smell benzene or another aromatic, it is because small amounts of the substance have floated away and are touching the inside of our nose!

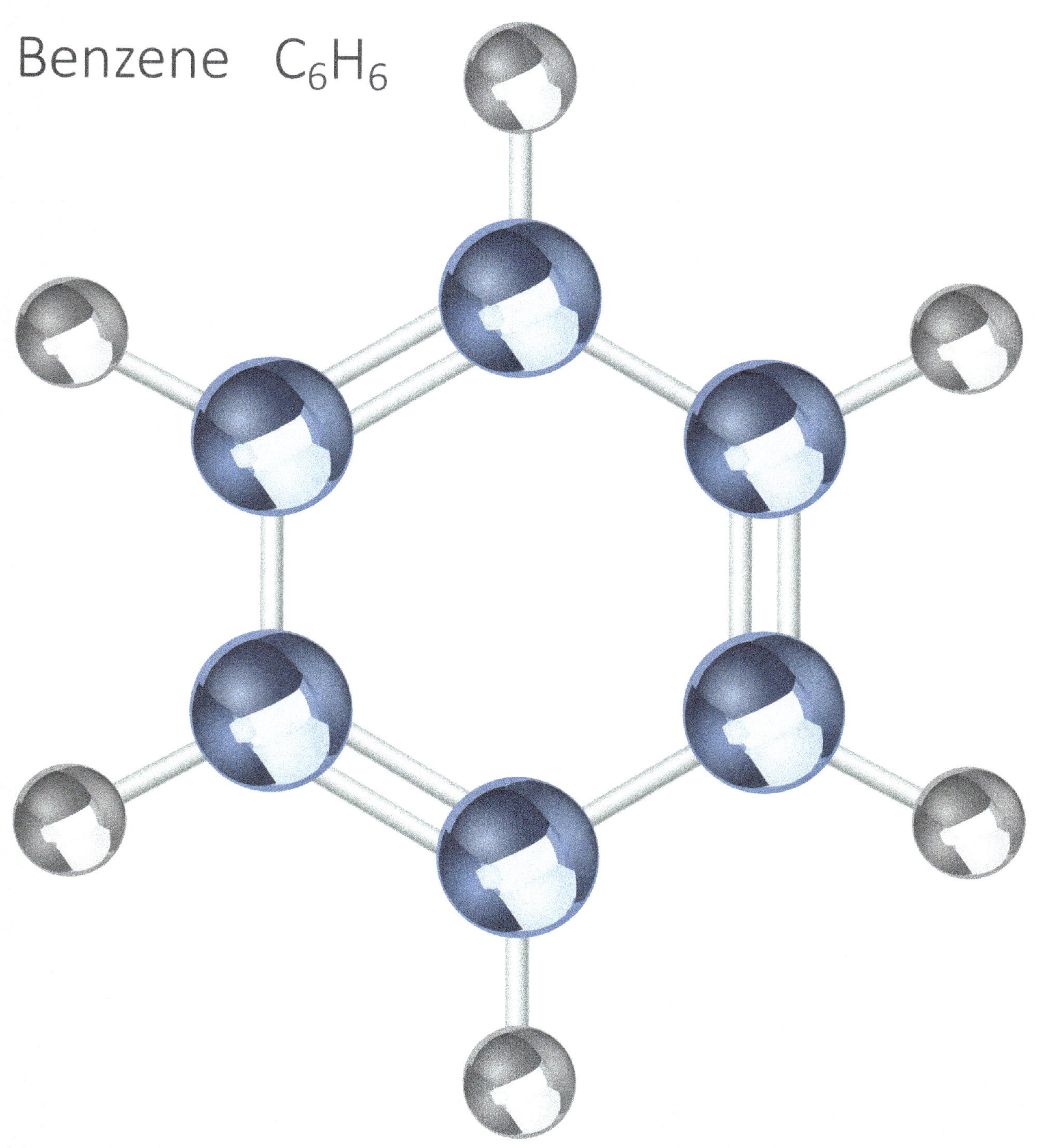

Benzene C6H6

WHAT WE MAKE FROM CARBON

In our world we rely on the strength and adaptability of carbon-based molecules for many things.

WARMTH

At a very basic level, when you burn wood in a campfire, you are enjoying the fact that the carbon-based molecules in the wood create light and heat when they transform by burning.

Camp fire at night

Weaving of cotton fabric

WEARABLES

When we wear clothing that is partly a natural fiber, like cotton, and partly a synthetic, we are wearing clothes made from two types of carbon-based compounds.

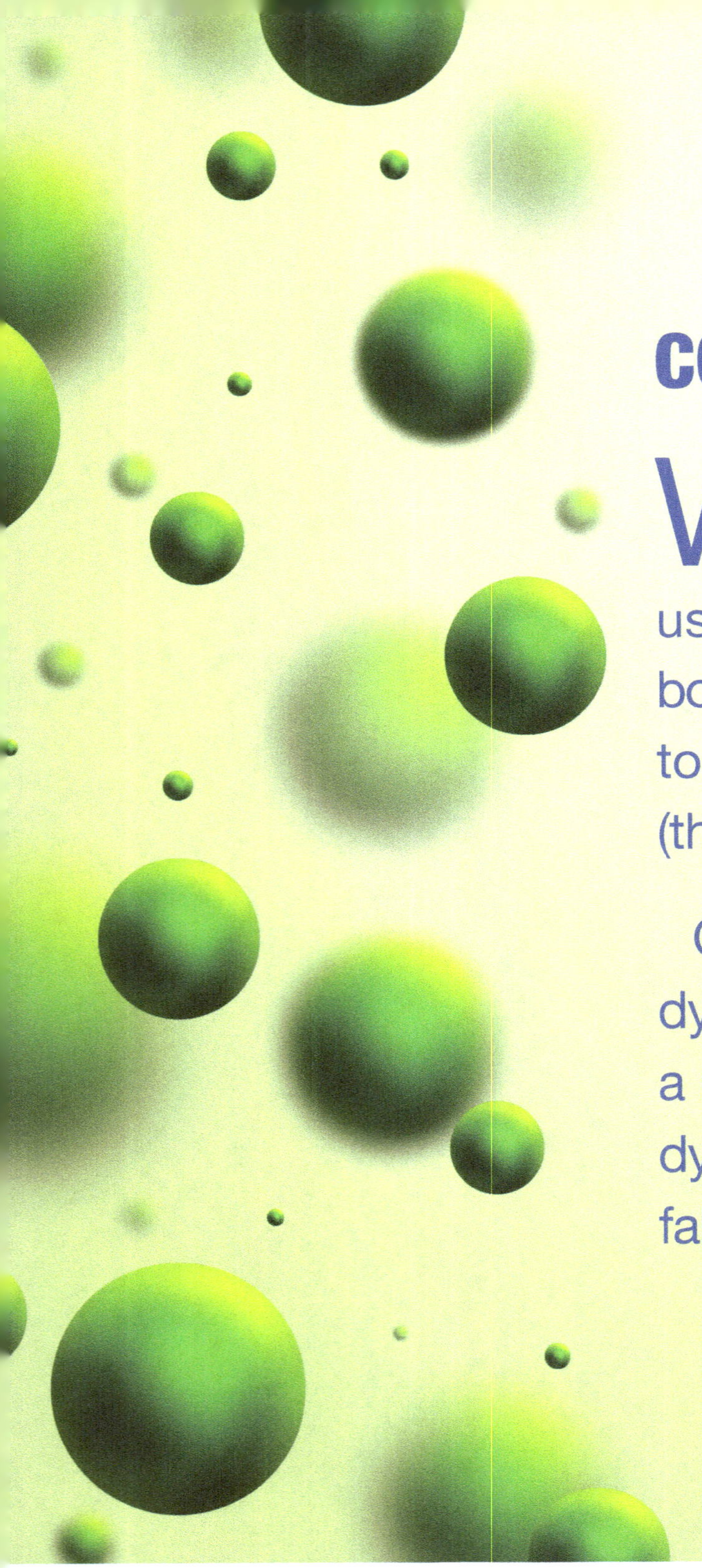

COLOR

When we paint a painting or a house, a lot of the time we are using carbon-based compounds both to create the colors we see and to create the way we deliver them (the tube of oil paint or the crayon).

Color can be in a pigment or a dye. Pigments go on the surface of a material, while the molecules of dyes bond with the molecules of the fabric to change its color.

Colorful piles of powdered dyes

Colorful plastic bags

PLASTICS

Our modern world uses plastics everywhere, from footwear to floor coverings to the packages we store food in. All plastics are carbon-based compounds. They are processed from fossil fuels like natural gas, coal, and oil. The molecules of plastics are called polymers, long chains of carbon atoms.

CARBON FIBER

Modern technology can make a sort of fabric by weaving long strands of carbon-based molecules together. The material is strong and very light, and it is easy to work with. Then we can cut and shape the sheets of fabric into amazing things, from car bodies to bicycles to space ships!

Carbon fiber composite raw material

We can make a bicycle body and then fill it with a chemical substance called a resin and bake the two together. This makes the frame of your bike stronger than steel, but at the same time much lighter.

Bicycle frame

MEDICINES

Scientists and doctors can make medicines that help us get better when we are sick by combining carbon-based compounds to respond to whatever it is that makes us sick. Sometimes these compounds are like, or just a little different from, what our body produces naturally.

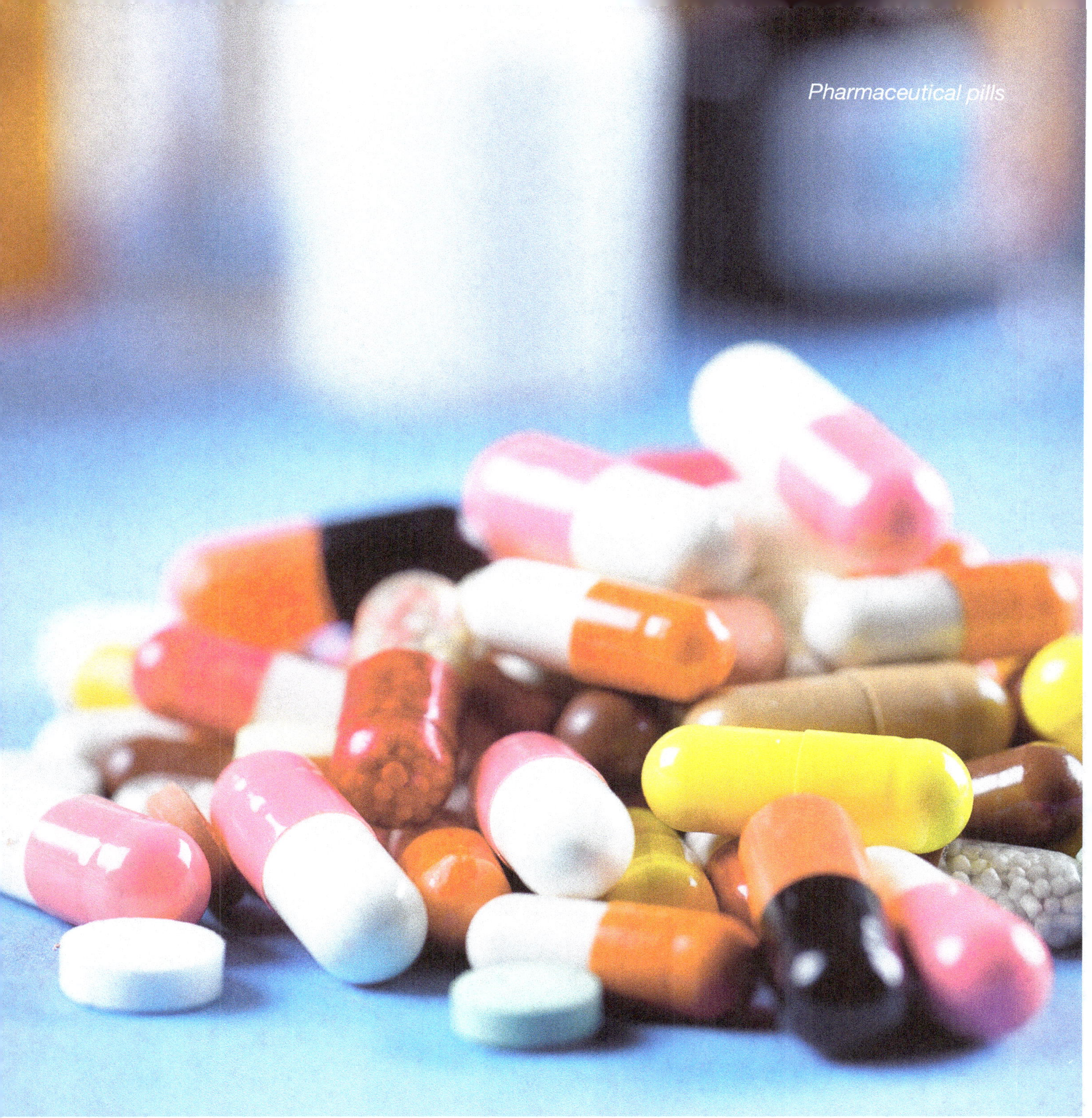
Pharmaceutical pills

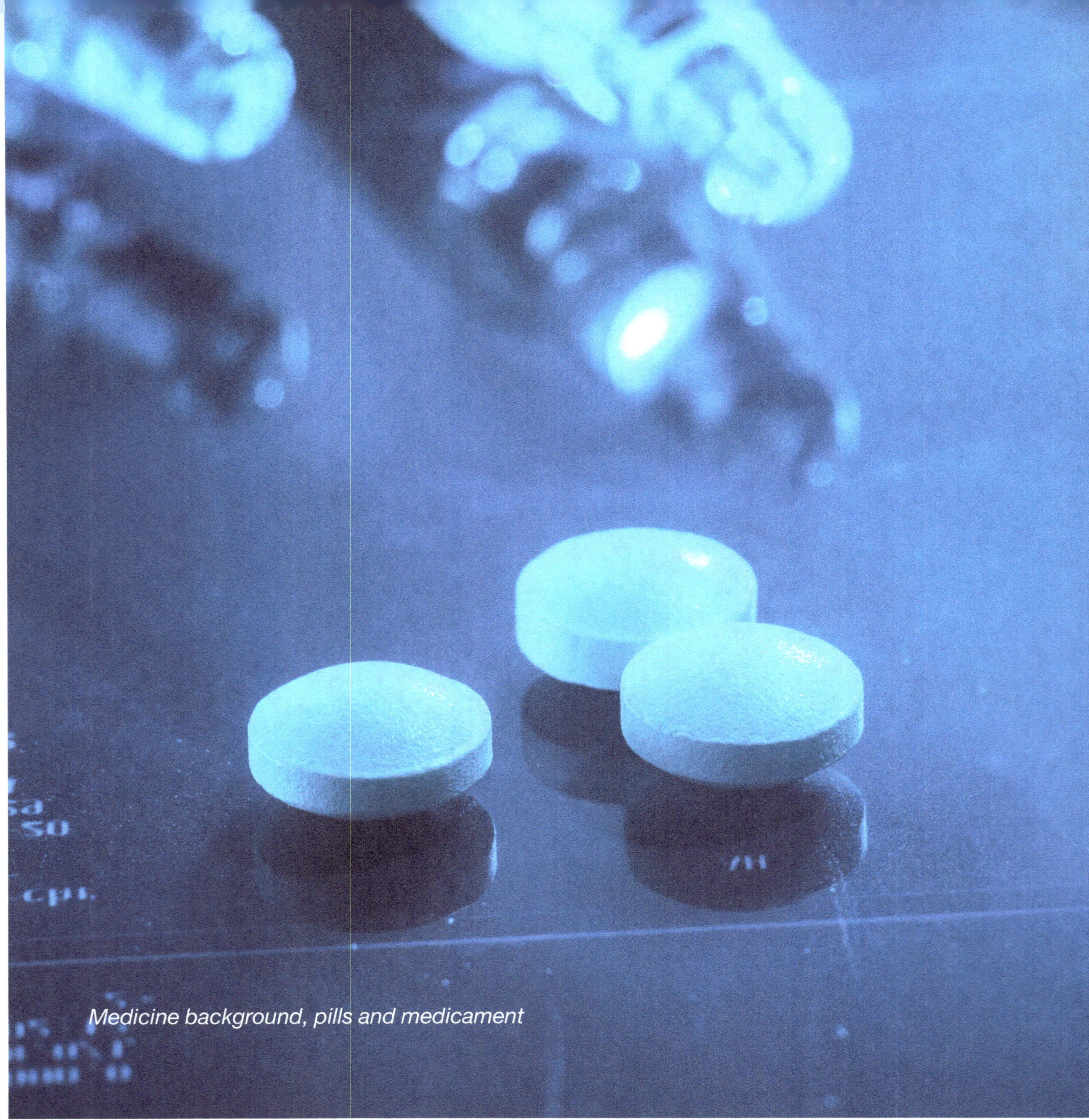
Medicine background, pills and medicament

Those who develop new medicines test them carefully to make sure they will not cause unexpected harm while providing their intended good!

A CARBON-BASED WORLD!

All life on Earth depends on some basic elements. Among them, hydrogen, oxygen, and carbon are the most important. Read on in other Baby Professor books, like *Peeling the Earth like an Onion* and *A Giant Shield: A Study of the Atmosphere*, to see what other surprises the Earth can show you!

Visit
BABY PROFESSOR
EDUCATION KIDS
www.BabyProfessorBooks.com
to download Free Baby Professor eBooks
and view our catalog of new and exciting
Children's Books